FISHING WISDOM

Insights from the Water's Edge

FISHING WISDOM

Insights from the Water's Edge

JOHN BALTISBERGER

amber
BOOKS

MIX
Paper | Supporting responsible forestry
FSC® C017606

Amber Books Ltd
United House
North Road
London N7 9DP
United Kingdom
www.amberbooks.co.uk
Facebook: amberbooks
YouTube: amberbooksltd
Instagram: amberbooksltd
X(Twitter): @amberbooks

ISBN: 978-1-83886-719-5

Design & Editorial: Amber Books Ltd

Printed in China

TRADITIONAL CHINESE BOOKBINDING

This book has been produced using traditional Chinese bookbinding techniques, using a method that was developed during the Ming Dynasty (1368–1644) and remained in use until the adoption of Western binding techniques in the early 1900s. In traditional Chinese binding, single sheets of paper are printed on one side only, and each sheet is folded in half, with the printed pages on the outside. The book block is then sandwiched between two boards and sewn together through punched holes close to the cut edges of the folded sheets.

Contents

Introduction

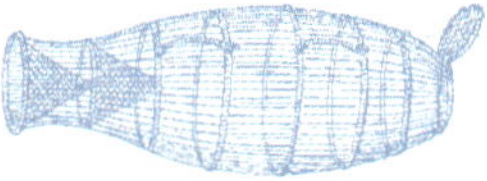

I remember fishing with my grandfather in a small bayou offshoot in Sour Lake, on the border of Louisiana and Texas. I had a piece of dry bamboo that I had tied a bit of string to, and on the other end of the string was a piece of sandwich meat. I was not having very much luck, for some reason. As I sat there tossing my bait in the water, two older men approached us. They spoke in heavy Mexican accents, marvelling at the small child trying to catch fish without a hook. After a few moments of watching me, one of the older men handed me one of his rods.

Awe in my eyes, I cast ... and immediately got tangled. I didn't catch anything that morning, but it made me aware of something, an unspoken community that existed, a family tied together by a love for fishing. I spent the summers out in Sour Lake, trawling ditches for crayfish and catching minnows in the shallows.

It wasn't until I was an adult and took my family to the coast that I rediscovered the magic of fishing. The first time I hooked a 15lb (6.8kg) (black drum and fought for my life to wrestle the 40in (101cm) fish (okay maybe it was 32in, or 78cm) into the boat, I was exhilarated. I caught a fish, not just a fish, a REAL fish. Not just a real fish, a fish I could eat. We filleted it and had a fish fry that night. There was something about eating food I had actually caught that was almost primal. I had hunted my own food. I had taken from the ocean and provided for my loved ones. It was almost spiritual, really. And it stood in stark contrast to the actual experience of fishing. A meditative stance in the surf or on the deck or dock, standing still as the world seemed to slow down around me. Only the lapping of waves, the sound of the breeze, and the call of sea birds intruding on the silence of the moment.

Because there is a Zen to fishing. A quiet peace that comes from the connection of rod to line to water. For many, it is the first steps towards parental bonding, the first tentative steps to finding our place within the natural world. From there, it balloons ... into a hobby, into a passion, into a livelihood. It is the connective tissue that links us to our ancestors through the oldest form of agriculture that has allowed us not only to survive but to thrive all over the globe.

Whether it was to feed their families, provide for their communities, or just get away from their overbearing bosses for a weekend, fishing has always been here for us. Over the centuries, many great thinkers have turned their minds and words towards the art of fishing. Here within are just a few of those words.

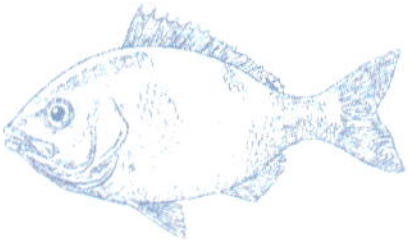

"Fishing is not just a hobby; it's a state of mind."

– Mariano Rivera

"To go fishing is the chance to wash one's soul
with pure air, with the rush of the brook,
or with the shimmer of sun on blue water."

– Herbert Hoover

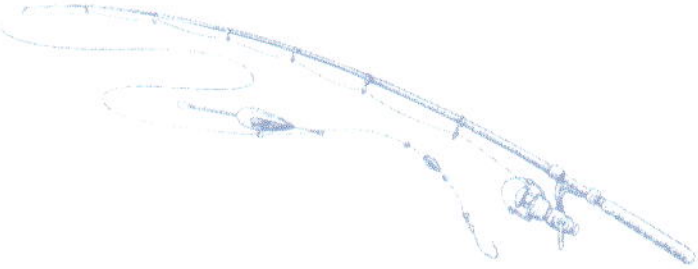

"There is certainly something in angling that tends to produce a serenity of mind."

– *Washington Irving*

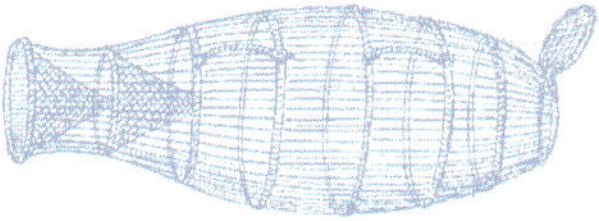

"Fishing is a constant reminder that control is an illusion, and acceptance is wisdom."

– *Unknown*

"Fly fishing is a contemplative experience that embodies the truth of nature and the nature of life."

– *Michael Vincent Stagnitta*

"Many men go fishing all of their lives without knowing that it is not fish they are after."

– Henry David Thoreau

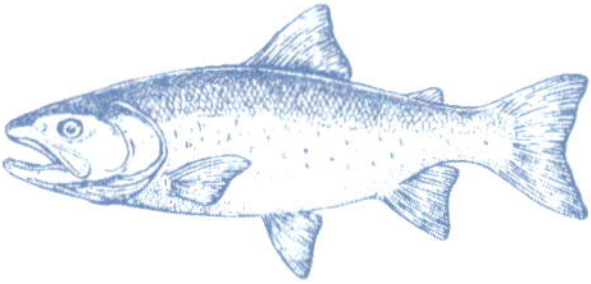

"Fishing is not an escape from life, but often a deeper immersion into it."

– Harry Middleton

"Some go to church and think about fishing,
others go fishing and think about God."

– Tony Blake

"The fishing is good in troubled waters."

– *German proverb*

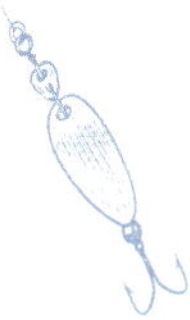

"Fishing brings out the reverence of the harmony of all things."

– *Ted Trueblood*

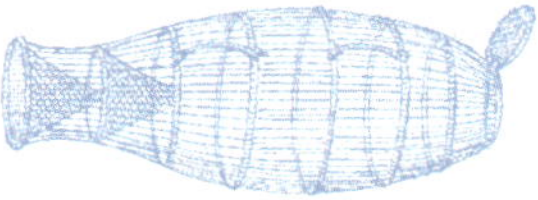

"I used to like fishing because I thought it had some larger significance. Now I like fishing because it's the one thing I can think of that probably doesn't."

–John Gierach

"Fishing is a hard job and a good job, it's a rich man's job and a poor man's job, it's a happy job and a sad job, it's a lot of things. But most of all it's a rewarding job."

– *Tom Brokaw*

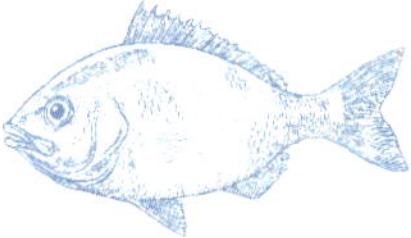

"Fishing is fundamentally a game of chance,
and at heart we are all gamblers."

– Dorothy Noyes Arms

"I've gone fishing thousands of times in my life, and I have never once felt unlucky or poorly paid for those hours on the water."

– William Tapply

"It is impossible to grow weary of a sport that is never the same on any two days of the year."

– *Theodore Gordon*

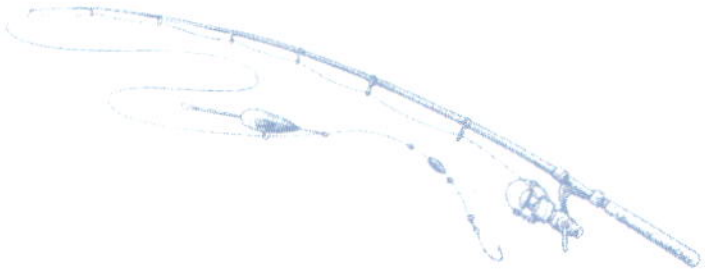

"I think I fish, in part, because it's an anti-social, bohemian business that, when gone about properly, puts you forever outside the mainstream culture without actually landing you in an institution."

–John Gierach

"Fishing is a lot like life. Sometimes, you just need to let it be and let it happen."

– *Unknown*

"Fishing is a discipline in the equality of men – for all men are equal before fish."

– *Unknown*

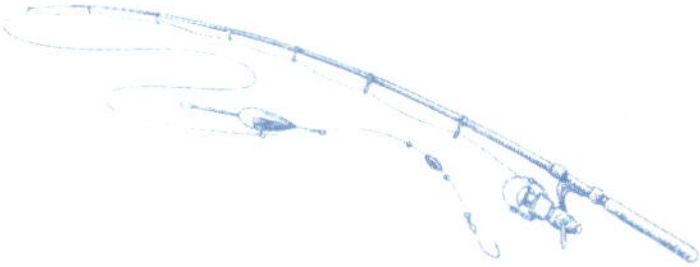

"... as the old saying goes: if you teach a man to fish, he will feed himself for a lifetime. But if you just give him a fishing pole, he'll have to teach himself."

– Zechariah Barrett

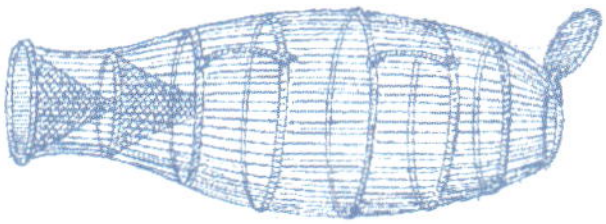

"The charm of fishing is that it is the pursuit of what is elusive but attainable, a perpetual series of occasions for hope."

– John Buchan

"Fishing is a way to forget the world and all its troubles."

– *Unknown*

"To fish for one's food is meditation."

– Jessica Marie Baumgartner

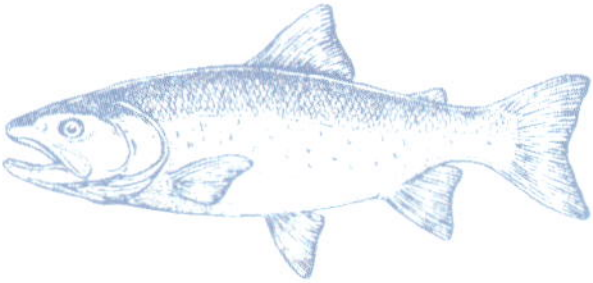

"I go fishing for reasons other than catching fish."

– Fennel Hudson

"Many who enjoy unspoiled places, wild creatures, and wild fish, are not idealists, but simply cognizant of the past greed and follies of man."

– David Stuver

"The best time to go fishing is when you can get away."

– Robert Traver

"Fishing is the art of doing almost nothing…
and loving every minute of it."

– *Unknown*

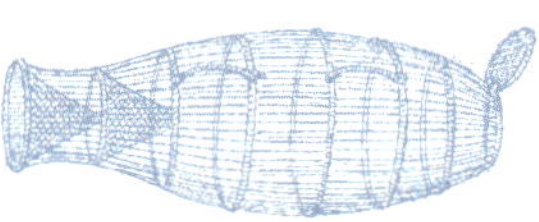

"I am firmly convinced that the ideal combination leading to a happy life is to have the time to both fish and read."

– Brian Murphy

"Angling is extremely time-consuming.
That's sort of the whole point."

– Thomas McGuane

"Three-fourths of the Earth's surface is water, and one-fourth is land. It is quite clear that the good Lord intended us to spend triple the amount of time fishing as taking care of the lawn."

– *Chuck Clark*

"Many of the most highly publicized events of my presidency are not nearly as memorable or significant in my life as fishing with my daddy."

–Jimmy Carter

"If fishing is a religion, fly fishing is high church."

– Tom Brokaw

"Many of us probably would be better fishermen
if we did not spend so much time watching and waiting
for the world to become perfect."

– Norman Maclean

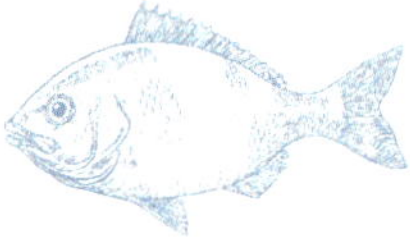

"The angling fever is a very real disease and can only be cured by the application of cold water and fresh, untainted air."

– Theodore Gordon

"The water you touch in a river is the last of that which has passed, and the first of that which is coming; thus, it is with time."

– Leonardo da Vinci

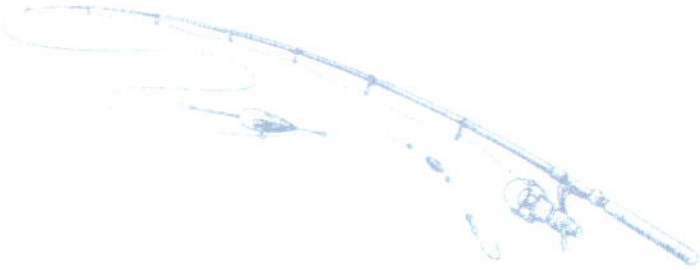

"What I liked about fishing at the break of day was to be a spectator to the whole of nature gently arousing itself from sleep."

– Craig D. Lounsbrough

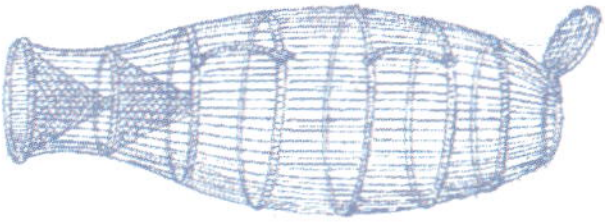

"All Americans believe that they are born fishermen. For a man to admit a distaste for fishing would be like denouncing mother-love or hating moonlight"

– John Steinbeck

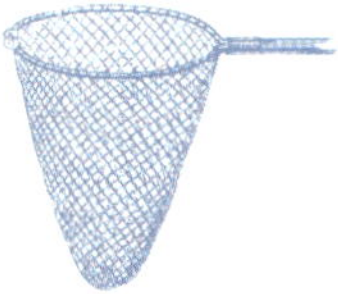

"Catching a fish is always secondary to the privilege of being able to put a line in the water."

– *Craig D. Lounsbrough*

"One thing becomes clearer as one gets older and one's fishing experience increases, and that is the paramount importance of one's fishing companions."

–John Ashley-Cooper

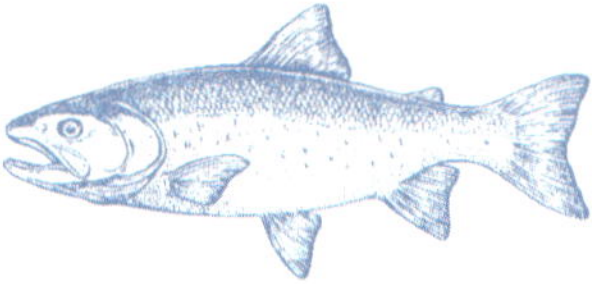

"The two best times to fish is when it's rainin' and when it ain't."

– Patrick F. McManus

"Listen to the sound of the river and you will get a trout."

– Irish proverb

"There is no greater fan of fly fishing than the worm."

– Patrick F. McManus

"I love fishing. You put that line in the water and you don't know what's on the other end. Your imagination is under there."

– Robert Altman

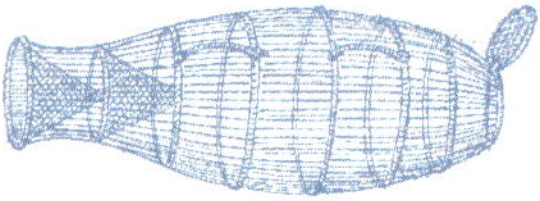

"A fisherman's skill is born from moments of stillness and patterns of movement."

– Bryant McGill

"Angling is a way of calming the soul and setting the spirit free."

– Dave Hughes

"Whether I caught fish or not, just the thrill of rolling out that line and watching my fly turn over has been good enough for me."

– *Curt Gowdy*

"In silence and patience, the wisdom of fishing unfolds."

–Julian Barnes

"There are only two occasions when Americans respect privacy. Those are prayer and fishing."

– Herbert Hoover

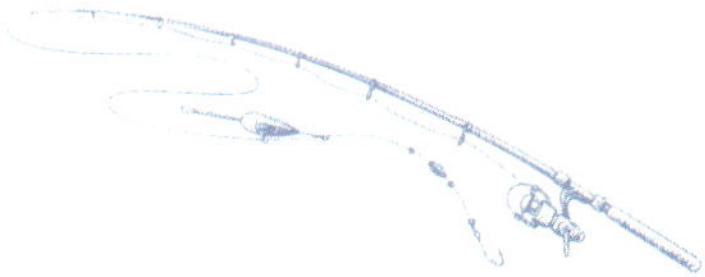

"Something to think about: If you fish the wrong fly long and hard enough, it will sooner or later become the right fly."

–John Gierach

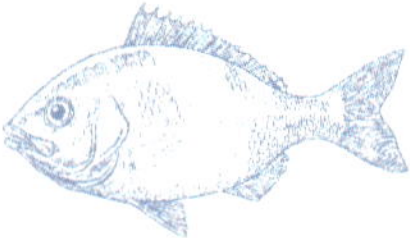

"A trout is a moment of beauty known only to those who seek it."

– Arnold Gingrich

"Most of the world is covered by water.
A fisherman's job is simple:
Pick out the best parts."

– Charles Waterman

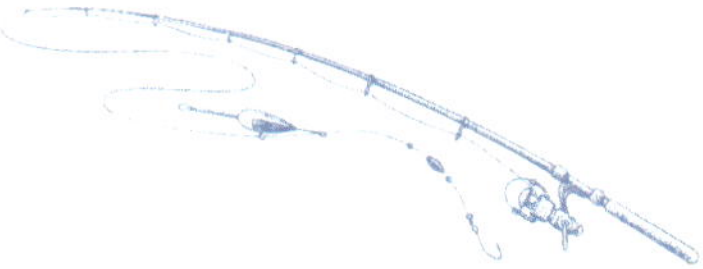

"Never throw a long line when a short one will serve your purpose."

– Richard Penn

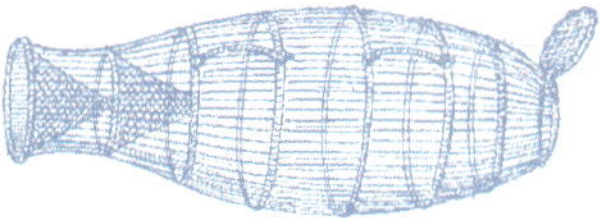

"Well, with fishing, you should hold the rod like it's part of your body. Become one with it."

– Kenneth Eade

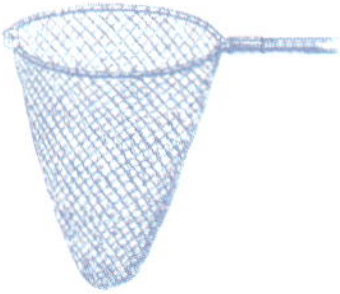

"Fishing provides time to think, and reason not to. If you have the virtue of patience, an hour or two of casting alone is plenty of time to review all you've learned about the grand themes of life."

– Carl Safina

"You can learn more from your failures than your successes when it comes to fishing."

– *Gary Borger*

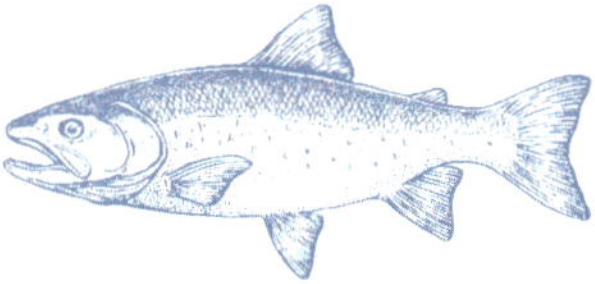

"You tickle trout by gaining their confidence, and then abusing it."

– *Robert A. Heinlein,* Glory Road

"To catch a fish is to hold a small piece of the wild in your hands."

– Unknown

"'We caught him,' I said. 'That's the fun part.' For us, at least. I doubt the fish would agree."

– *Kathy Reichs*

"The fish and I were both stunned and disbelieving to find ourselves connected by a line."

– *William Humphrey*

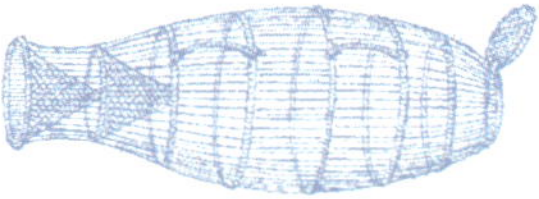

"There's no taking trout with dry breeches."

– Miguel de Cervantes

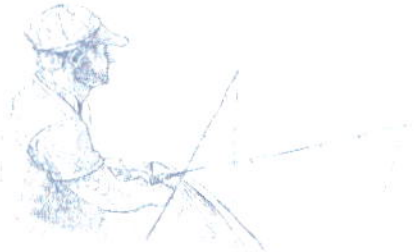

"If I fished only to capture fish, my fishing trips would have ended long ago."

– Zane Grey

"He who wants to catch fish must not mind getting wet."

– Spanish proverb

"If catching fish is your only objective, you are either new to the game or too narrowly focused on measurable results."

– David Stuver

"It has always been my private conviction that any man who pits his intelligence against a fish and loses has it coming."

– John Steinbeck

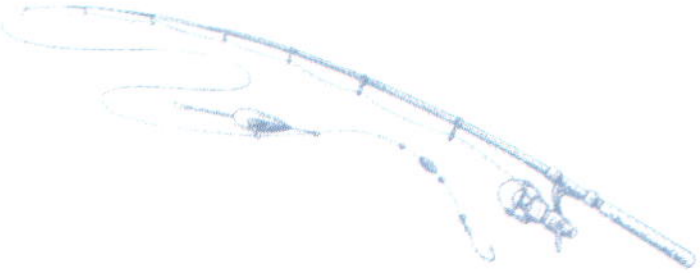

"Grant me the Serenity to accept the size of the fish
I catch, the Courage not to lie about it,
and the Wisdom to know that none of my fishing buddies
would believe me anyway."

– Fisherman's prayer

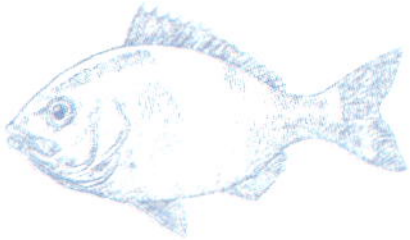

"May the holes in your net be no larger than the fish in it."

– Irish blessing

"The angler forgets most of the fish he catches, but he does not forget the streams and lakes in which they are caught."

– Charles K. Fox

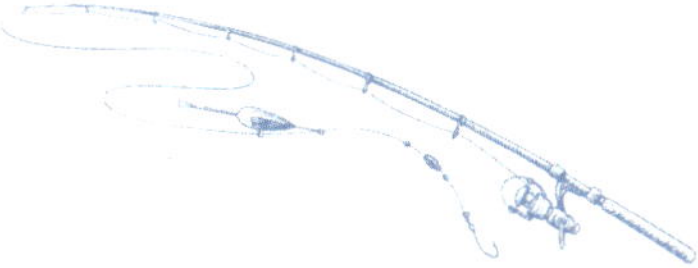

"In every species of fish there is a story."

– William Thackeray

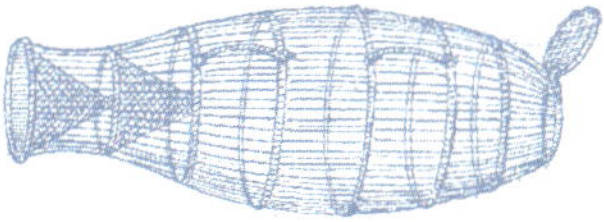

"Catching fish is low on my agenda when I go fishing.
I'm much more interested in savoring the day
and exploring the wildlife of the river."

– Fennel Hudson

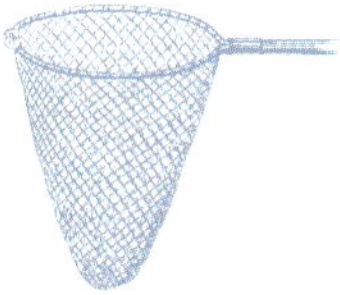

"I didn't catch a fish today, but I did catch a tree, a log, and my own hat."

– Unknown

"When your bait goes missing without a nibble, you start to wonder if fish have group chats about avoiding you."

– *Unknown*

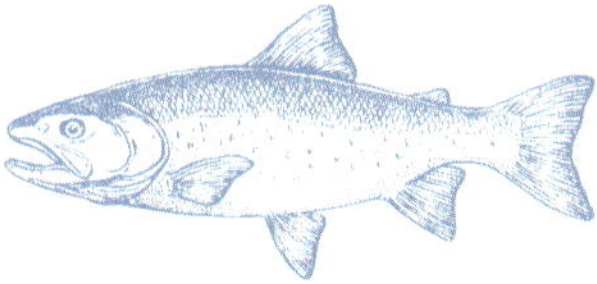

"Fishing is like dating; it's all catch and release until you find a keeper."

– Unknown

"He liked fishing and seemed to take pride in being able to like such a stupid occupation."

– *Leo Tolstoy*, Anna Karenina

"Writers fish for the right words like fishermen fish for, um, whatever those aquatic creatures with fins and gills are called."

–Jarod Kintz, '94,000 Wasps in a Trench Coat'

"The man who coined the phrase 'Money can't buy happiness' never bought himself a good fly rod!"

– Reg Baird

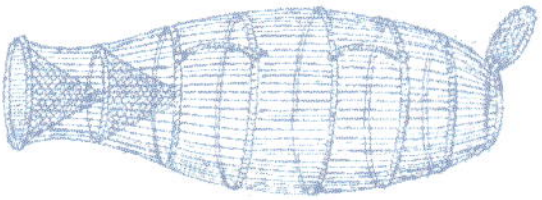

"Teach a man to fish and you've fed him for a lifetime. Unless, of course, he doesn't like sushi – then you'll have to buy him a Kelly Kettle, hobo stove and frying pan as well."

– Fennel Hudson, 'Fly Fishing: Fennel's Journal No. 5'

"Fishermen are born honest, but they get over it."

– Ed Zern, 'To Hell with Fishing'

"The fishing was good; it was the catching that was bad."

– A.K. Best

"There's a fine line between fishing and standing on the shore looking like an idiot."

– Steven Wright

"Most fishermen swiftly learn that it's a pretty good rule never to show a favorite spot to any fisherman you wouldn't want to be married to."

– John Gierach

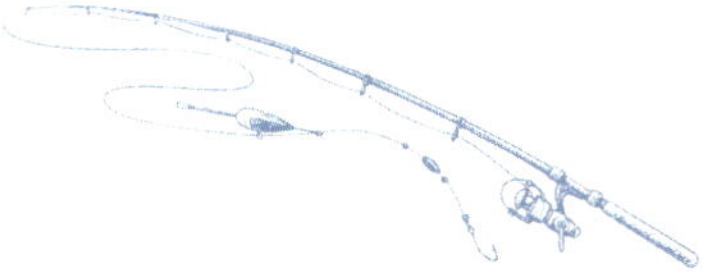

"Fishing is like sex. When it is great, it is great. When it is bad, it is still great."

– *Unknown*

"Life is just a series of obstacles preventing you from fishing."

– *Unknown*

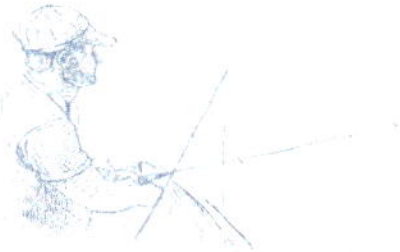

"Do not tell fish stories where the people know you. Particularly, don't tell them where they know the fish."

– Mark Twain

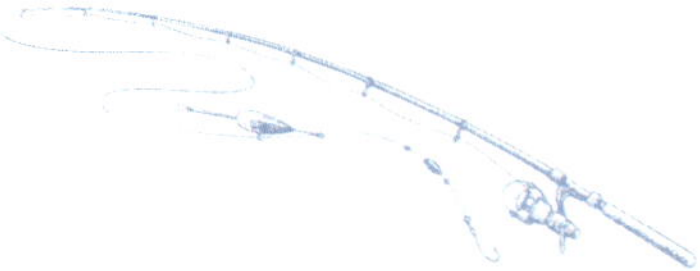

"If people concentrated on the really important things in life, there'd be a shortage of fishing poles."

– Doug Larson

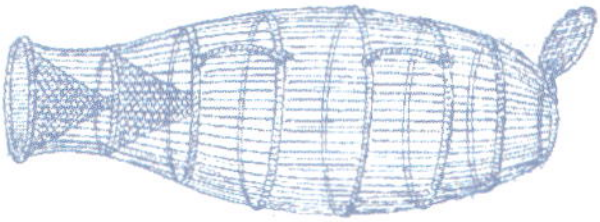

"All fishermen are liars; it's an occupational disease with them like housemaid's knee or editor's ulcers."

– Beatrice Gray Cook

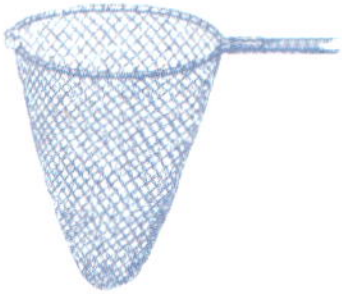

"I am not against golf, since I cannot suspect it keeps armies of the unworthy from discovering trout."

– Paul O'Neil

"Our tradition is that of the first man who sneaked away to the creek when the tribe did not really need fish."

– Roderick Haig-Brown

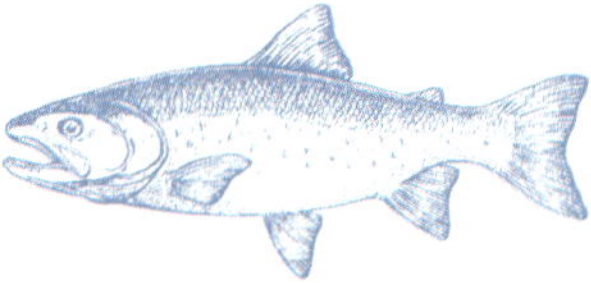

"I don't want to sit at the head table anymore.
I want to go fishing."

– George Bush

"So long, and thanks for all the fish."

– Douglas Adams

Picture Credits

Alamy: 28 (adsR), 30 (Mark Conlin), 72 (Michelle Bridges), 87 (SuperStock)

Art Institute of Chicago: 8, 48

Birmingham Museums Trust: 51

Boston Public Library: 49

Cleveland Museum of Art: 9, 31, 32, 73, 95

Dreamstime: 10 (Kalinski), 19 (Adeliepenguin)

Getty Images: 7 (Geoffrey Clements/Corbis/VCG), 11 (Historica Graphica Collection), 13 (duncan1890), 20 (GraphicaArtis), 21 (ilbusca), 33 (Bettmann), 34 (Heritage Images), 35 (Underwood Archives), 36 & 37 (ilbusca), 38 (A&J Fotos), 47 (George Pickow), 54 (H. Armstrong Roberts/ClassicStock), 55 (GraphicaArtis), 56 (Photo Josse/Leemage), 57 (DEA/ICAS94), 58 (ilbusca), 59 (DEA/ICAS94), 60 (Clu), 61 (ilbusca), 62 (duncan1890), 70 (Science & Society Picture Library), 71 (Photo Josse/Leemage), 74 (Print Collector), 75 (Bettmann), 77 (Archive Photos), 81 (ClassicStock), 82 (DEA/Biblioteca Ambrosiana), 83 (Heritage Images), 84 (H. Armstrong Roberts/ClassicStock), 85 (DEA/Biblioteca Ambrosiana), 88 (Heritage Images), 94 (eclipse_images)

The J. Paul Getty Museum, Los Angeles: 86

Library of Congress: 14, 23, 42, 43, 45, 63, 64, 65

Metropolitan Museum of New York: 12, 40, 50, 52, 67

Minneapolis Institute of Art: 24, 44, 89

Musée Carnavalet, Paris: 41

Rijksmuseum, Amsterdam: 16, 22, 25, 27, 39, 46, 53, 68, 69, 90

Pxhere: 15, 26

Wellcome Collection: 18, 66, 78, 80, 91

Yale Center for British Art: 29, 76, 92, 93

Yale University Art Gallery: 17, 79